United States Army
Shoulder Patches
and Related Insignia

United States Army Shoulder Patches and Related Insignia

From World War I to Korea

1st Division to 40th Division

William Keller

Schiffer Military History
Atglen, PA

Acknowledgments

My sincerest gratitude goes out to all that helped and made the production of this volume possible. Namely Dan Alloggio, Kurt H. Andariese, David S. Angle, Peter M. Bennethum, Gary Castellino, Rocco Collura, David Fisher, Mike Furey, Scott Glemby, Bob Ford, Richard T. Graney, Daniel Griffin, Kurt Keller, Wayne T. Mc Cabe, Bruce J. Pitre Jr., Gus Radle, James F. Rudy, Garth Thompson, Charles Van Der Eems, Robert A. Wilson and John B. Wright. Without any of whom this book would not have been as complete or accurate. I wish to commend them for their hospitality and cooperation. It was a unique privilege to be invited to view their collections and photograph the best each had to offer. Without exception, each visit was a wonderful learning experience. Their dedication not just to collecting but the preservation of history made this project a joy to work on and the photographs contained within speak volumes to the lifetime commitment it has been for many of them. I'm especially grateful to the individuals who graciously provided me with identification for some of the more unusual pieces. One last note, I would like to especially thank those brave souls who mailed me photos and patches to photograph.

To all the soldiers who served, both remembered and forgotten.

Book design by Robert Biondi.
Principal photography by Kurt Keller; additional photography by William Keller.
Dust jacket photo by Robert Biondi.

Printed in China.
ISBN: 0-7643-1394-0

We are always looking for people to write books on new and related subjects. If you have an idea for a book, please contact us at the address below.

Published by Schiffer Publishing Ltd.
4880 Lower Valley Road
Atglen, PA 19310
Phone: (610) 593-1777
FAX: (610) 593-2002
E-mail: Schifferbk@aol.com.
Visit our web site at: www.schifferbooks.com
Please write for a free catalog.
This book may be purchased from the publisher.
Please include $3.95 postage.
Try your bookstore first.

In Europe, Schiffer books are distributed by:
Bushwood Books
6 Marksbury Ave.
Kew Gardens
Surrey TW9 4JF
England
Phone: 44 (0)208 392-8585
FAX: 44 (0)208 392-9876
E-mail: Bushwd@aol.com.
Free postage in the UK. Europe: air mail at cost.
Try your bookstore first.

Contents

Use Guide and Abbreviation Key

Use this section as a quick reference point for the manufacturing style codes listed in the captions. For ease of use, each Division will be its own chapter. Within each chapter each photo caption will contain all the information about each patch. After the patch number, the period the patch is from is listed. This is followed by the Country of origin and, if unique beyond the divisional identity, the identification of the patch and finally the construction description. All patches without a country listed, with the exception of World War I's are believed to be made in the United States. Information not covered by the introduction will be discussed in the caption when the topic is reached – see the following sample entry:

Fig. 8.16. Post World War II, Germany. Bullion and felt. Translation: 8th Division, Patch 16, manufactured after World War II, made in Germany, bullion and felt construction.

Bullion = Any spun, woven or wrapped metallic thread.

CS = Chain Stitch: Two top threads attached to base material by a single pick up or backing thread. Under close examination this embroidery type resembles a chain. This technique is usually done with a hand guided embroidery machine. A hand embroidered technique also exists that resembles this stitch pattern.

DI = Distinguished Unit Insignia: Metal insignia with enameled or painted designs commonly found for regimental units. Occasionally these can be found in miniature patch form for wear on Garrison caps, lapels and shoulder straps.

ET = Embroidered on twill: Any patch where exposed twill base material is part of the design of the patch.

FE = Fully embroidered: The embroidery covers the entire surface of the patch.

Felt = Pressed woolen material that has no weave.

HE = Hand Embroidered: The design of the patch is embroidered with needle and thread by hand.

ME = Machine embroidered: The design is embroidered on material with a machine guided by a prepared pattern.

ODB = Olive Drab Border

TM = Patch is believed to be theater made but is of an unknown origin.

Wool = Wool that is a woven cloth with or without texture.

? = The possibility exists that the patch is from this period or country of origin.

Introduction

Soon after the arrival of the U.S. Army in any theater of War or Occupation, local merchants catered to the soldiers, who passed through or were stationed there. Anything from scarves for mother, to cups and plates emblazoned with insignia could be bought by the by the Doughboy and GI alike. As you will note by the great variety in this book, patches were also on the list. The U.S. Army usually provided the soldier with enough patches for each of his service uniforms whether they were domestically produced or not. Often the nicest patches worn were ones made "In Theater" which were beautifully hand embroidered or made with bullion thread. Many individuals purchased theater made insignia on their own, in some cases for souvenirs or for wear on a dress uniform. Sometimes patches were bought in theater simply to replace ones that were worn out or lost. In many cases these patches were strictly against the regulations or approved for local wear only. Occasionally the soldiers added their own touches to the design of a patch with the addition of special tabs that reflected a unit's nickname or a numerical designation. Like other theater made insignia, these to were usually unofficial.

This volume, the first in a series, will hopefully paint a fairly complete picture of the development and evolution of Shoulder Sleeve Insignia or the Shoulder Patch and related insignia of the U.S. Army. The starting point of the series are the Divisional Shoulder patches, as they were the first units to adopt patches during and after World War I. Through the gallery of photographs, I hope this series will effectively document the many variations and manufacturing styles of the periods covered and the countries that produced them. Every effort has been made to include interesting and unique insignia to demonstrate the diversity that can be found. There will be something for every reader to enjoy, regardless of specific or general interest.

This series will follow a general format as to the period that each patch was made in. They will consist of World War I, which covers 1918 to approximately 1923 and the end of the Occupation of Germany. The next will be the Interwar period that includes the 1920s until just before World War II. The third period covered will be World War II, which consists of just the war years, 1941-1945. The final era featured will be Post World War II which includes the German and Japanese Occupations and the Korean War era.

You may note that the World War I patches are only labeled as "World War I". This is done because patches from this era were manufactured in France or Germany and still others were made in the U.S. and shipped overseas. Without proper provenance, it is sometimes difficult to determine with any certainty the exact country of origin. As a general rule of thumb a majority of the hand made patches were made in France. Some personnel had their insignia made in Germany during the occupation and some had their patches made in America. The 81st Division for example arrived in France wearing a shoulder patch. However, French or German materials are not a guarantee that the patch is from that country. With the War Reparations imposed on Germany, materials and machines of all manner were turned over to the Allies. With this in mind, it is conceivable to have patches made in France using German machines and material. Thus, to avoid error, all World War I patches are simply classified as "World War I". With patches made at a later date this problem does not usually exist because units can be easily traced to areas of service or veterans may have been available to answer questions. From this a good base of comparison can be mapped out to identify other insignia of the same origin. Unfortunately, in many cases, identification of the manufacturer is somewhat of an "art" at best, and as such, it is more subjective than absolute. Case in point, how to tell the difference between a patch made in Germany compared with that of Austria. Within each era patches of similar styles are grouped together regardless of chronological age. While this is mainly done out of convenience, it would be difficult to arrange the patches in an order that accurately reflects the true age of all insignia covered. It should be noted that every attempt has been made to weed out any spurious or reproduction items. To the best of anyone's knowledge, only genuine period pieces are pictured. This is not solely my opinion, but also that of the contributors who were more than helpful in that regard. For approval dates of the patches and general unit history, the reader should refer to *Shoulder Sleeve Insignia of the U.S. Armed Forces 1941-1945* by Smith & Pelz, which is the best guide for this information. One final note, in some cases there may be a lack of variety for some of the units. This may be due to the short service life of a unit or the unavailability of a patch or patches for photography. With that said, I hope that you will get as much enjoyment from reading this volume as I did from assembling it.

Bill Keller
July 15, 2000

• • •

The Civil War

The story of the shoulder patch begins in 1918 with the departure of the 81st "Wildcat" Division from the U.S. for the Great War. While this is a fairly well known fact, little attention is paid to the original use of cloth insignia by the U.S. Armed Forces. In 1862 under the direction of General Philip Kearny, the first such badge was adopted for use. The original purpose was to aid in the identification of his troops in battle but it became much more than that. In time, it became a source of unit pride and badge of honor, a tradition that continues today. It consisted of little more than a small square of red flannel worn upon the kepi. General Kearny sacrificed one of his own blankets to begin the production of these devices. After the effectiveness of this simple measure was demonstrated, the entire Union Army adopted the concept and created over twenty different such "Corps Badges". They came in a variety of colors to designate different divisions within each Corps. Red for the 1st Division, white for the 2nd, and blue for the 3rd. Occasionally a tri-color device was used for headquarters and some Corps added a 4th division, which was distinguished by green. The style of manufacture varied widely from simple felt cutouts to jeweler quality badges made from silver and gold.

Fig. 1. General Philip Kearny. Courtesy of Wayne T. McCabe.

Fig. 2. Captain J. B. Winslow wearing a cloth and bullion 5th Corps Badge. Courtesy of Wayne T. McCabe.

Fig. 3. Captain David Ayers, 5th and later 7th New Jersey Volunteer Infantry Regiment wearing a metal 3rd Corps Badge. Courtesy of Wayne T. McCabe.

Fig. 4. Captain George V. Boutelle's forage cap with 3rd Corps, 2nd Division cloth badge. Capt. Boutelle was part of the 2nd New York Volunteer Infantry Regiment and wore this cap at the Battle of Chancellorsville.

Fig. 5. 2nd Corps Artillery Headquarters badge made of bullion and cloth.

Fig. 6. 1st Veteran Army Corps (Hancock's) gunstock inlay Corps badge.

Fig. 7. Gold 17th Corps badge that belonged to Private William G. Nichols, Co. H, 76th Illinois Volunteer Infantry Regiment.

The Spanish-American War

After the Civil War the use of Corps badges waned and not until 1898 and the Spanish-American War was the U.S. Army again directed to use a set of badges to distinguish the different Corps. As originally intended these were to be made of felt just like their predecessors and worn on the hat or breast. The badges of this period vary from simple painted metal stampings to ornate hand crafted works of art produced by the nation's most renowned jewelers.

Fig. 9. Stamped and painted 1st Corps, 3rd Division Badge.

Fig. 10. 5th Corps Headquarters enamel on bronze badge made by Bailey Banks & Biddle.

Fig. 8. Cabinet Card of an unidentified Spanish-American War soldier wearing a metal 3rd Corps Badge on his hat.

World War I
1918-1923

During World War I the shoulder patch was born, starting a trend that continues today. While most of the shoulder patches were approved for wear before the end of the war, the majority were not worn until after the Armistice. The 81st Division was among the few units that did wear a shoulder patch before the cessation of hostilities. Like their Corps badge predecessors, many of the first patches were simply felt or wool cut to shape. Other construction types are featured in figures 12 to 14; these represent the majority of the styles made during this period. One of the most unique styles from this period is the "Liberty Loan" patch, which was made in conjunction with the War Loan program. These are of a woven construction, made with the same technique as a modern shirt label.

Fig. 11. Die cut wool 28th Division shoulder patch.

Fig. 12. Service of Supply. Wool on wool construction.

Fig. 13. Service of Supply. Hand embroidered on wool.

11

Fig. 14. District of Paris. Bullion on wool.

Fig. 15. Reverse of 7th Division Liberty Loan style patch.

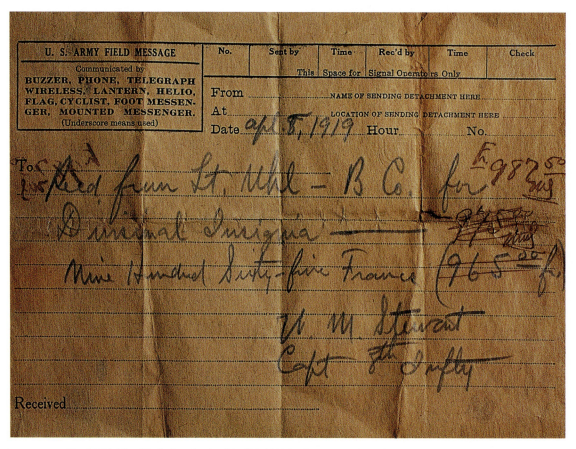

Fig. 16. Divisional Insignia order dated April 8, 1919 for Company B, 8th Infantry Regiment, 8th Division.

The Interwar Period
1924-1940

Patches from this era were made in much the same way as they were during World War I except the designs are more refined, standardized and the quality is much improved. During this period the twill patch was introduced. They are almost universally manufactured on khaki cotton twill and were intended to be worn on the summer weight uniform. They have either thin emboidered borders or the edge is folded under to form a border. Patches of the same design can be found embroidered on Officer's dark olive drab wool elastique and on olive drab wool for enlisted personnel. Also worth noting are patches made on dark blue wool for wear on the dark blue dress jacket which was worn for a short time after World War I and then again just before World War II. All patches of this period were made in the United States or a U.S. Territory.

Fig. 17. Interwar period 2nd Infantry Division patch. This example features a hand embroidered Indian on a wool star which is applied to a wool background.

Fig. 18. 8th Division patch machine embroidered on a wool background.

Fig. 19. 5th Corps twill patch.

World War II
1941-1945

At the outbreak of World War II the Interwar period patches were still being worn but the rapid buildup of U.S. forces dictated the need for conservation of wool. These new patches substituted cotton twill for wool as the base material. The designs were fully embroidered on the base material, completely covering it. These were then cut from the cloth right up to the edge of the patch, trimming away all base material. For this reason these are often referred to as "cut edge" patches. A characteristic of some of the early World War II patches is the Olive Drab or "OD" border. For many of the World War II patches this feature is a constant but for others it is a scarce and highly desirable trait from a collectors point of view. Another variation that enjoys some following among collectors is the "greenback" or the use of OD thread on the back of the patch. It is believed that this practice was discontinued sometime in the mid war years to save OD thread for other applications. This seems to be borne out by the approval dates of some of the later formed Infantry Divisions and the absence of greenback patches for these units. Another type of patch from this era is the non OD border. These feature a color other than OD as the border color, where OD is normally used. Still another type of fully embroidered U.S. made insignia from this period are patches with khaki colored borders, presumably for wear on the summer uniforms. The final type worth noting are twill patches. Unlike the Interwar era khaki twill patches, the small number of World War II patches made this way usually feature exposed twill that is the background color of the design.

Fig. 20. 88th Division patch with an olive drab border

Fig. 22. The reverse of two different 27th Division "Greenback" patches.

Fig. 21. Standard World War II fully embroidered 88th Division patch.

Italian Theater Patches

One of the first major Theaters of involvement for the U.S. that was capable of producing insignia was Italy. The construction style of hand embroidered Italian patches in many ways mimics that of Italian military insignia with many of the same materials being used. These patches often use a template or underlayment as a base for the design being embroidered. The colors of the thread used often have a "soft" or pastel look. Another type of patch made in Italy is a machine woven variety. These are characterized by a "mirror" reverse in which the front colors are reversed on the back.

Fig. 23. Italian made Allied Forces patch hand embroidered on a satin background. Although this example is in poor condition, it nonetheless illustrates perfectly the characteristics of many Italian made patches including the cardboard underlay and the pastel coloring.

Fig. 24. Front of Italian made woven style Allied Forces shoulder patch.

Fig. 26. Italian made bullion Africa-Italy tab.

Fig. 25. Back of **Fig. 24** showing the color reversal of this type of patch.

English Made Patches

The English are probably better known for the plethora of U.S. Army Air Corps insignia they produced during the war but they too made patches for the Army. These patches vary most notably from their American made counterparts in that they are usually thinner in cross section and the colors used are softer and have a glassy, almost translucent appearance. Another key difference is the English version of olive drab, which is a much lighter shade, closer to a tan or "coffee" color. Like U.S. made patches these have also been observed with colored backs, most often black, but also pink, gold, and orange.

Fig. 27. Side by side comparison of English and US made patches. Left: English made 9th Air Force patch. Right: U.S. made 9th Air Force patch.

Fig. 28. English made Iceland Base Command showing the light border color.

Fig. 29. English made colored back HQ ETOUSA, Com Z (2nd design) patches.

German Occupation Patches

Like other countries, Germany used many of the same materials and styles to produce insignia for U.S. military personnel that it had used for its own armed forces. This can be clearly seen by comparing any of the higher quality hand made insignia that were made for either army. Often the types of cord bullion are the same as used on Officer's eagles and collar tabs. Another common material used most notably in the borders of patches is "Cello" a form of nylon that has a yellow or gold appearance. Occasionally soutache, a type of colored piping cord used on the front of German caps, is found on the edge or used in the design of the patch. Machine embroidered German patches have a distinctive "salt and pepper" or "loopy" look to their backs. Another feature present in some is a "slant" to the rows of embroidery that usually runs diagonally in the patch. One other form that can be found is the woven patch. These patches are manufactured with a rayon front and are usually attached to a cloth backing. The term "Bevo" is often used to refer to these woven insignia because of the similarity to wartime German insignia made by this company. While this is useful as a collectors term for woven insignia, the trade name Bevo actually refers only to insignia made by the firm Bevo-Wuppertal from the city of Wuppertal-Barmen which was destroyed during the war.

Fig. 30. German made 7th Army hand embroidered on wool using "Cello" cording and thread.

Fig. 32-33. Above and below: Front and reverse of German made fully embroidered 28th Division patch.

Fig. 31. World War II SS-Gruppenführer collar tab. The US equivalent for this rank is Lieutenant General. This tab was used from 1942 until 1945. Notice the similarity of the construction styles with **Fig. 30.**

Fig. 34. Reverse of German made fully embroidered 7th Division patch.

Fig. 35. German made woven 1st Division patch.

Japanese Occupation Patches

Unlike the other countries featured, Japan has a history of embroidery dating back hundreds of years and some of the finest embroidery ever created can be found on kimonos and temple robes of the past. This tradition was carried into the 20th century and led to the production of some of the most beautiful examples of shoulder patches ever made. Figures 38 to 40 show some of the hand made types that can be found. The fine cross-stitching seen on many of the earlier hand made patches emulates the fine work of centuries past. This stitch pattern is not only decorative; it also adds strength and durability to the patch. The backs of some of these patches often feature scrap kimono cloth. Machine made Japanese patches are characterized by the irregular look of their designs. Lines are not always straight, edges are not always square and lettering has a somewhat jagged appearance. These features stem from the use of hand guided embroidery machines. These patches, as with hand made versions, are almost universally made of silk.

Fig. 36. Japanese gift cloth, c.1750. Silk and bullion embroidery on silk.

Fig. 37. Japanese souvenir embroidery, c.1950. Silk and bullion embroidery on silk.

Fig. 38. Navy Amphibious Forces, Japanese made, fully hand embroidered.

Fig. 39. 1st Marine Air Wing, Japanese made, hand embroidered on silk.

Fig. 40. GHQ Honor Guard, Japanese made, quilted silk and bullion construction.

Fig. 41. VA-95 novelty Squadron patch dated 1953, Japanese made, hand guided machine embroidered.

Fig. 42. Reverse of **Fig. 41** showing embroidery pattern.

Korean Made Patches

Korean made patches in many ways resemble Japanese made patches but they usually appear cruder and less refined, and are often made of different materials. Coarse wool is generally used as the base material whether the patch is machine or hand made. Sometimes present is a backing material which resembles a fabric softener dryer sheet. The most common Korean made patch and the one most familiar to the collector, is the souvenir or "tour" jacket patch. The use of a hand guided embroidery machine can be clearly seen in figures 43 to 45.

Fig. 43. Korean Communication Zone, Korean made hand guided machine embroidered on wool.

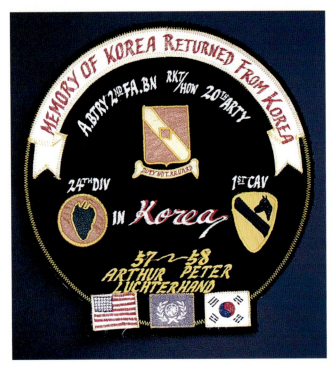

Fig. 44. 24th Division/1st Cavalry Division, Korean made souvenir jacket patch, part applied, part hand guided machine embroidered construction.

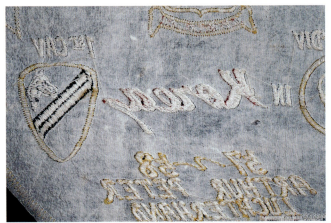

Fig. 45. Reverse of **Fig. 44**, showing detail of construction style and the unique backing material.

United States Army
Shoulder Patches and Related Insignia

1st Division to 40th Division

Fig. 1.1. World War I. An unidentified 1st Division, 5th Artillery Regiment Doughboy wearing a wool on wool patch.

Fig. 1.2. World War I. An unidentified Doughboy wearing a 1st Division patch without a background shield.

Fig. 1.3. World War I. Shieldless felt 1st Div. Patch.

Fig. 1.4. World War I. Variant wool "1" machine applied to woven shield.

Fig. 1.5. World War I. Variant wool "1" machine applied to German uniform wool shield.

Fig. 1.6. World War I. ME on wool.

Fig. 1.7. World War I. Liberty Loan.

Fig. 1.8. World War I. An unidentified Doughboy wearing standard World War I style 1st Division patch.

Fig. 1.9. World War I. Variant tall shield. This type has been observed with the top of the shield sewn next to the shoulder seam of the jacket. Wool on wool.

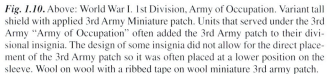

Fig. 1.10. Above: World War I. 1st Division, Army of Occupation. Variant tall shield with applied 3rd Army Miniature patch. Units that served under the 3rd Army "Army of Occupation" often added the 3rd Army patch to their divisional insignia. The design of some insignia did not allow for the direct placement of the 3rd Army patch so it was often placed at a lower position on the sleeve. Wool on wool with a ribbed tape on wool miniature 3rd army patch.

Fig. 1.11. Above right: World War I. Variant 1st Division with added red border. Wool on wool.

Fig. 1.12. Right: World War I. 1st Division patch with added "D". The meaning of this is unknown. Felt on wool.

Fig. 1.13. World War I. 28th Infantry, Company D "Canteen" decorated with 1st Division insignia.

Fig. 1.14. Interwar. Thin "1" variation. Felt on felt.

Fig. 1.15. Interwar. Thin "1" variation. Felt on felt with applied cloth backing.

Fig. 1.17. Interwar. Felt on felt variation with beige colored shield.

Fig. 1.16. Interwar. An unidentified 1st Division, 26th Infantry Regiment soldier wearing a wool on wool patch.

Fig. 1.18. Interwar. ME on coarse wool.

Fig. 1.19. Interwar. ME on wool with ME border.

Fig. 1.20. Interwar. ME on folded edge wool shield.

Fig. 1.21. Interwar. Felt on folded edge wool shield.

Fig. 1.22. Interwar. ME on twill.

Fig. 1.23. Interwar. Wool on folded edge twill shield.

Fig. 1.24. Interwar. Felt on folded edge wool shield.

Fig. 1.25. Interwar. HE on coarse felt shield.

Fig. 1.26. Interwar?/Post World War II TM?. HE on Officer's wool "Pinks" material with folded edge shield.

Fig. 1.27. Interwar. Felt on folded edge twill shield.

Fig. 1.28. Interwar. Wool on folded edge waterproof cotton duck shield.

Fig. 1.29. Interwar/World War II. ME on wool with ME border.

Fig. 1.30. Interwar/World War II. ME on twill.

Fig. 1.31. World War II. FE with added HE details.

Fig. 1.32. World War II, Italy. HE on satin with HE border.

Fig. 1.33. World War II, England. FE.

Fig. 1.34. Post World War II, Germany. FE.

Fig. 1.35. Post World War II, Germany. FE.

Fig. 1.36. Post World War II, Germany. ME on wool with ME border.

Fig. 1.37. Post World War II, Germany. ME on wool with ME border and HE decoration.

Fig. 1.38. Post World War II, Germany. ME on wool with ME border. Beige shield variation.

Fig. 1.39. Post World War II, Germany. HE on felt.

Fig. 1.40. Post World War II, Germany. HE on felt with ME border.

Fig. 1.41. Post World War II, Germany. HE on twill.

Fig. 1.42. Post World War II, Germany. HE on wool with bullion decoration and red cord border.

Fig. 1.43. Post World War II, Germany. HE on felt with bullion decoration and twisted bullion cord edge.

Fig. 1.44. Post World War II, Germany. HE on felt with bullion decoration and woven bullion cord edge.

Fig. 1.45. Post World War II, Germany. Plastic injection molded 1st Division cigarette case dated 1945.

Fig. 2.1. World War I. Unidentified 1st Division doughboy and Private Dunbar, 2nd Division, 12th Field Artillery Regiment. In World War I the 2nd Division utilized a series of shaped backgrounds for each Regiment and color coded the background for different units within each regiment. For the largest units in the Division the color code is Black for Headquarters Companies, Red for the 1st Battalion, Yellow for the 2nd Battalion, Blue for the 3rd Battalion, Purple for Machine Gun Companies and Green for Supply Companies.

Fig. 2.2. World War I. 2nd Division, Army of Occupation. Hand painted Indian applied to velvet shield with HE and bullion miniature 3rd Army patch.

Fig. 2.3. World War I. Liberty Loan.

Fig. 2.4. World War I. Unidentified 2nd Division, 9th Infantry Regiment doughboy with a friend from the 12th Field Artillery. This is the first pattern of the 9th Infantry Regiment's patch that is similar to the design of the 23rd Infantry Regiment.

Fig. 2.5. World War I. Charles Portcales wearing a first pattern 9th Infantry patch.

Fig. 2.6. World War I. Charles Portcales wearing the more familiar second pattern pentagon shaped 9th Infantry patch.

Fig. 2.7. World War I. 9th Infantry Regiment, 1st Battalion. ME on wool Indian and star applied through a wool background. A standardized Indian and star combination was machine embroidered on an olive drab wool base. This patch was usually added to a shaped and colored background to designate the different units in the division.

Fig. 2.8. World War I. 9th Infantry Regiment, 2nd Battalion. Painted Indian applied to wool.

Fig. 2.9. World War I. 9th Infantry Regiment, 3rd Battalion. ME on wool Indian and star applied to wool.

Fig. 2.10. World War I. 9th Infantry Regiment, 3rd Battalion. ME on wool Indian and star applied to HE pentagon.

Fig. 2.11. World War I. 9th Infantry Regiment, 3rd Battalion. Wool Indian with HE details on a wool star and pentagon.

Fig. 2.12. World War I. Unidentified 2nd Division, 23rd Infantry Regiment, 1st Battalion doughboy.

Fig. 2.13. World War I. 2nd Lieutenant Thomas W. Timpson's 2nd Division, 23rd Infantry Regiment shoulder patch. Lt. Timpson was a Silver Star winner in World War I.

Fig. 2.14. World War I. Liberty Loan style 23rd Infantry Regiment patch.

Fig. 2.15. World War I. 23rd Infantry Regiment, Headquarters Company. Painted Indian applied to wool.

Fig. 2.16. World War I. 23rd Infantry Regiment Headquarters Company. ME Indian and star applied to wool base.

Fig. 2.17. World War I. 23rd Infantry Regiment, 1st Battalion. Painted Indian applied to wool base.

Fig. 2.18. World War I. 23rd Infantry Regiment, 1st Battalion. ME Indian and star applied to wool base.

Fig. 2.19. World War I. A group of unidentified 23rd Infantry Regiment, 2nd Battalion (yellow background) doughboys.

Fig. 2.20. World War I. Unidentified 23rd Infantry Regiment medical Sergeant.

Fig. 2.21. World War I. 23rd Infantry Regiment, 3rd Battalion. Wool on wool with HE embroidered details.

Fig. 2.22. World War I. 23rd Infantry Regiment, 3rd Battalion. Wool on wool with HE details.

Fig. 2.23. World War I. 23rd Infantry Regiment, 3rd Battalion. ME Indian and star on velvet.

Fig. 2.24. World War I. 23rd Infantry Regiment, 3rd Battalion. Painted Indian on wool.

Fig. 2.25. World War I. Sergeant Leo A. Rowley's 23rd Infantry Regiment, Machine Gun Company patch. Painted Indian on velvet.

Fig. 2.26. World War I. Another one of Sergeant Leo A. Rowley's patches, this one wool on wool with HE details.

Fig. 2.27. World War I. 23rd Infantry Regiment, Supply Company. Wool on wool with HE details.

Fig. 2.28. World War I. 23rd Infantry Regiment, Supply Company. ME Indian and star on wool.

Fig. 2.29. World War I. 2nd Division, 5th Marine Regiment, 1st Battalion. HE Indian applied to wool base with bullion soutache border.

Fig. 2.30. World War I. 2nd Division, 5th Marine Regiment, 1st Battalion. Liberty Loan patch modified and applied to wool.

Fig. 2.31. World War I. Unidentified 5th Regiment, 2nd Battalion Marine.

Fig. 2.32. World War I. 5th Marine Regiment, 3rd Battalion. Painted Indian applied to wool.

Fig. 2.34. World War I. 6th Marine Regiment, 2nd Battalion. ME Indian and star applied to wool. Orange is substituted for yellow in this patch.

Fig. 2.33. World War I. Unidentified 6th Regiment, 2nd Battalion Marine.

Fig. 2.35. World War I. Private Dunbar 12th Field Artillery Regiment.

Fig. 2.36. Left: World War I. Corporal Preston R. Hille, 12th Field Artillery Regiment.

Fig. 2.37. World War I. Corporal Hille's 12th Field Artillery Regiment, 2nd Battalion patch. ME Indian and star applied to wool.

Fig. 2.38. Below: World War I. Corporal Hill and Private Dunbar with a group of friends. Notice the 12th Field Artillery Regiment Patch is being worn as a pocket patch on the shirt.

Fig. 2.39. World War I. 12th Field Artillery Regiment, 3rd Battalion. ME Indian and star applied to wool.

Fig. 2.40. World War I. Unidentified 2nd Division, 15th Field Artillery Regiment Doughboy.

Fig. 2.41. Left: World War I. Another nice image of two unidentified 15th Field Artillery Regiment doughboys.

Fig. 2.42. World War I. 15th Field Artillery Regiment, 2nd Battalion. ME Indian and star applied to wool.

Fig. 2.43. World War I. 15th Field Artillery Regiment, 3rd Battalion. Wool Indian with HE details applied to cotton star on wool base.

Fig. 2.45. World War I. 17th Field Artillery Regiment, 1st Battalion. Painted on silk Indian applied through wool star on wool base.

Fig. 2.46. World War I. Unidentified 17th Field Artillery Regiment doughboy.

Fig. 2.44. World War I. Two unidentified "mascots" of the 17th Field Artillery Regiment.

Fig. 2.47. World War I. 17th Field Artillery Regiment, 1st Battalion. ME Indian and star applied to wool.

Fig. 2.48. World War I. 17th Field Artillery Regiment, 3rd Battalion. Painted Indian applied to wool.

Fig. 2.49. World War I. 5th Machine Gun Battalion. Wool Indian with HE details applied to cotton star on wool base.

Fig. 2.50. World War I. 5th Machine Gun Battalion. Wool Indian with HE details applied to wool star and base.

Fig. 2.51. World War I. Unidentified 6th Machine Gun Battalion Marine.

Fig. 2.52. World War I. 6th Machine Gun Battalion. Wool Indian with HE details applied to wool star with soutache border on velvet background.

Fig. 2.54. World War I. 2nd Engineer Regiment, 1st Battalion. ME Indian and star applied to wool.

Fig. 2.53. World War I. Unidentified 2nd Engineer Regiment doughboy.

Fig. 2.55. Right: World War I. 2nd Engineer Regiment, 1st Battalion. Painted Indian applied to a velvet background.

Fig. 2.56. World War I. 2nd Engineer Regiment, 2nd Battalion. ME Indian and star applied to felt.

Fig. 2.57. World War I. Unidentified 2nd Division Sanitary Train doughboy.

Fig. 2.58. World War I. Sam Mull, 2nd Division Sanitary Train.

Fig. 2.59. World War I. 2nd Division Sanitary Train. Painted Indian applied to wool.

Fig. 2.60. World War I. 2nd Division, 1st Signal Battalion. Wool Indian with HE details applied to a wool star on a velvet shield.

Fig. 2.61. World War I/Interwar. 2nd Division Supply Train. HE Indian and star applied to a wool shield.

Fig. 2.62. World War I/Interwar. 2nd Division Supply Train. ME on wool.

Fig. 2.63. Interwar. HE Indian on wool star applied to wool shield.

Figs. 2.64 to 2.67. Interwar. ME Indian on felt applied to wool shield.

Fig. 2.68. Interwar. ME Indian and star on twill shield.

Fig. 2.69. Interwar?/World War II? 2nd Division, 23rd Infantry Regiment. FE.

Figs. 2.70 and 2.71. World War II. FE, ODB.

Fig. 2.72. World War II. ET, ODB.

Fig. 2.73. World War II. ET.

Figs. 2.74 and 2.75. Post World War II, Germany. FE, ODB.

Figs. 2.76 and 2.77. Post World War II, Germany. FE.

Fig. 2.78

Fig. 2.79

Figs. 2.78 to 2.81. Post World War II, Japan. FE.

Fig. 2.82. Post World War II, Japan. ME on silk with ME border.

Fig. 2.83. Post World War II, Japan. HE Indian on bullion star on felt shield with bullion edge.

Fig. 2.84. Post World War II, Japan. ME Indian on bullion star on felt shield with bullion border.

Fig. 2.85. Post World War II, Japan. Felt Indian with HE details and bullion headdress on a bullion star on wool shield.

Fig. 2.86. Post World War II, Japan. HE Indian with bullion details on bullion cloth star applied to a wool shield with a bullion edge.

Fig. 2.87. Post World War II, Germany. Right facing Indian ME on felt.

Fig. 2.88. Post World War II, Japan. Right facing Indian, FE. Right facing 2nd Division patches are intended to be worn on the right shoulder of the uniform. This ensures that the Indian has the appearance of always going foreword.

Fig. 2.89. Post World War II, Japan. 2nd Division Korea tab, ME on felt.

Fig. 2.90. Post World War II, Japan. 2nd Division Korea tab, HE on silk. Tabs like this were intended to be worn over the basic unit patch to indicate Korean War service.

Fig. 2.91. Post World War II, Japan/Korea. 2nd Division patch type DI. Blue background, screwback.

Fig. 3.1. World War I. Unidentified 3rd Division Signals doughboy.

Fig. 3.2. World War I. Wool on wool 3rd Division patch that belonged to an unidentified 7th Infantry Regiment doughboy.

Fig. 3.3. World War I. Cotton tape on wool.

Fig. 3.4. World War I. Ribbed tape on wool.

Fig. 3.5. World War I. Two unidentified 3rd Division, 10th Field Artillery Regiment doughboys.

Fig. 3.6. World War I. Felt on felt with embroidered border.

Fig. 3.7. World War I. ME on felt.

Fig. 3.8. World War I. Liberty Loan

Fig. 3.9. World War I. Unidentified 3rd Division NCO wearing a bullion tape and velvet style patch.

Fig. 3.10. World War I. Unidentified 3rd Division 1st Lieutenant wearing another version of a bullion and velvet patch.

Figs. 3.11 and 3.12. Above and below: World War I. Bullion tape on wool.

Fig. 3.13. World War I. Bullion tape on velvet.

Fig. 3.14. World War I. 3rd Division, Army of Occupation. Cotton on velvet with added HE bullion miniature 3rd Army patch.

Fig. 3.15. World War I. Unidentified 18th Field Artillery Regiment doughboy with a bullion and velvet patch.

Fig. 3.16. World War I. Alternate style World War I 3rd Division patch. ME on felt.

Fig. 3.17. Interwar. Felt on felt.

Fig. 3.18. Interwar. ME on felt.

Fig. 3.19. Interwar. ME on twill.

Fig. 3.20. World War II. Staff Sergeant Kenneth J. Brown, 3rd Division, 39th Field Artillery Regiment.

Fig. 3.21. World War II, Italy. Sergeant Brown's 3rd Division patch. HE on satin.

Fig. 3.22. World War II, Italy. HE on twill.

Fig. 3.23. World War II, Italy. Woven.

Fig. 3.24. World War II, Italy. Screen printed on satin with ME border.

Fig. 3.25. World War II/Post World War II, TM. Woven.

Fig. 3.26. Post World War II, Germany. HE on felt.

Fig. 3.27. Post World War II, Germany. HE on felt.

Fig. 3.28. Post World War II, Germany. Bullion on felt.

Fig. 3.29. Post World War II, Japan. ME.

Fig. 3.30. Post World War II, Japan. Felt and bullion on felt.

Fig. 3.31. Post World War II. 3rd Division, Third Pentomic Drill Team. "Pentomic" was an organizational structure adopted by the U.S. Army in 1956 to deal with the problems of an "Atomic" battlefield. FE patch with HE tab.

Figs. 3.32 and 3.33. Post World War II, Germany. Front and reverse of a 3rd Division, 15th Infantry souvenir token.

Fig. 4.1. World War I. Unidentified 4th Division doughboy wearing a wool on wool 4th Division patch.

Fig. 4.2. World War I. HE on wool.

Fig. 4.3. World War I. HE on wool.

Fig. 4.4. World War I. Liberty Loan.

Fig. 4.5. World War I. Unidentified 4th Division, 16th Field Artillery Regiment doughboy with an embroidered on wool patch.

Fig. 4.6. World War I. HE on wool.

Fig. 4.7. World War I. CS on wool.

Fig. 4.8. World War I. ME on ribbed cloth.

Fig. 4.9. World War I. 4th Division, Army of Occupation. Felt on wool with added ribbed cloth tape and wool 3rd Army miniature patch.

Fig. 4.10. World War I. 4th Division, Army of Occupation. HE on wool with added ribbed cloth tape and wool 3rd Army miniature patch.

Fig. 4.11. World War I. 4th Division, Army of Occupation. HE on wool.

Fig. 4.12. Left: World War I. Unidentified doughboy wearing a variant 4th Division shoulder patch. This example features ivy "arms" that form the number 4.

Fig. 4.13. Interwar. HE on felt.

Fig. 4.14. Interwar. ME on wool.

Fig. 4.15. Interwar. ME on twill.

Fig. 4.16. Interwar?/World War II. 4th Division, square style. FE

Fig. 4.17. Interwar?/World War II. 4th Division square style. ME on twill.

Fig. 4.18. World War II. Ribbed background variation. FE.

Fig. 4.19. World War II, England. 4th Division square style. FE.

Fig. 4.20. World War II, England. FE on wool.

Fig. 4.21. Post World War II, Germany. Five different 4th Division patches. FE/ME.

Fig. 4.22. Post World War II, Germany. HE on felt.

Fig. 4.23. Post World War II, Germany. FE patch with added bullion applied to black felt base.

Fig. 4.24. Post World War II, Germany. HE on felt with bullion detail and cord edge.

Fig. 5.1. World War I. Captain D.C. Schwartz wearing a simple felt cut out 5th Division patch on his overcoat.

Fig. 5.2. World War I. Felt on wool.

Fig. 5.3. World War I. ME on felt.

Fig. 5.4. World War I. HE bullion on felt.

Fig. 5.5. World War I. 5th Division, Army of Occupation ME on wool.

Fig. 5.6. Above: World War I. Oversized HE on wool 5th Division patch.

Fig. 5.7. Above right: World War I. Unidentified 5th Division Doughboy with felt or wool on wool patch.

Fig. 5.8. Right: World War I. Unidentified 5th Division NCO with felt patch. The lines you see on the image were added by the photographer to highlight the insignia.

Figs. 5.9. to 5.10. Interwar. Two different styles of ME on wool patches.

Fig. 5.11. Reverse of ***Figs. 5.9*** and ***5.10***

Fig. 5.12. World War II. FE.

Fig. 5.13. World War II. FE, ODB.

Fig. 5.14. Post World War II, Germany. Bullion on felt.

Fig. 5.15. Post World War II, Germany. Bullion on felt.

Fig. 5.16. Post World War II. Patch: FE. Tab: ME on twill.

Fig. 5.17. Post World War II, Germany. Painted patch type DI, spring pin.

Fig. 6.1. World War I. Unidentified 6th Division doughboy.

Fig. 6.2. World War I. Die cut wool.

Fig. 6.3. World War I. Hand cut wool.

Fig. 6.4. World War I. Unidentified 6th Division, 51st Regiment doughboy with variation 6th Division patch.

Fig. 6.5. World War I. Wool with added wool "6".

Fig. 6.6. World War I. Wool with added wool "6" applied to circular background.

Fig. 6.7. World War I. ME on felt.

Fig. 6.8. World War I. Wool with HE "6".

Fig. 6.9. World War I. Wool with HE "6".

Fig. 6.11. Interwar. Felt on wool.

Fig. 6.10. World War I. Two unidentified doughboys with 6th Division, Army of Occupation patches.

Fig. 6.12. Interwar. ME on wool.

Fig. 6.13. World War II. FE, ODB.

Fig. 6.14. World War II. FE, ODB.

Fig. 6.15. Post World War II, Germany. FE, ODB.

Fig. 6.16. Post World War II, Germany. Bullion on felt.

Fig. 6.17. World War II. Unidentified family of servicemen with a 6th Division Corporal at center.

Fig. 7.1. World War I. Unidentified 7th Division, 64th Infantry Regiment doughboy.

Fig. 7.2. World War I. Felt on felt.

Fig. 7.3. World War I. Wool on wool.

Fig. 7.4. World War I. ME on felt.

Fig. 7.5. World War I. ME on felt.

Fig. 7.6. World War I. Unidentified 7th Division doughboy with ME on felt or wool patch.

Fig. 7.7. World War I. ME on wool.

Fig. 7.8. World War I. Liberty Loan.

Fig. 7.9. Interwar. ME on wool.

Fig. 7.11. World War II /Post World War II. FE red border variation. This style was used during and after World War II.

Fig. 7.10. World War II. Unidentified 7th Division Technical Sergeant.

Fig. 7.13. World War II. FE, ODB.

Fig. 7.12. World War II. FE red border variant weave.

Fig. 7.14. World War II, England. Patches, such as this, can be found occasionally made in a theater where that unit did not serve. Often these patches were made for right shoulder wear. Veterans are allowed to wear the patch of the unit they served with in combat on the right shoulder if it is different than the unit they are currently serving with.

Fig. 7.15. Post World War II, Germany. FE. Notice how the hourglass extends to the border.

Fig. 7.16. Post World War II, TM. FE.

Fig. 7.17. Post World War II, Germany. HE on felt applied to wool.

Fig. 7.18. Post World War II, Germany. HE on felt with bullion border.

Fig. 7.19. Post World War II, Japan. FE.

Fig. 7.20. Post World War II, Japan. Felt on felt with bullion detail and border on felt base.

Figs. 7.21 to 7.24. Post World War II, Japan. Four different variations of felt on felt with bullion detail and border.

Fig. 7.25. Post World War II, Japan. HE with a quilted pattern hourglass on felt with bullion border.

Fig. 7.26. Post World War II, Japan. HE quilted background with bullion detail and border.

Figs. 7.27 and 7.28. Post World War II, Japan. Two different 7th Divisions, HE on wool with bullion detail and border with integral bullion "Korea" tab.

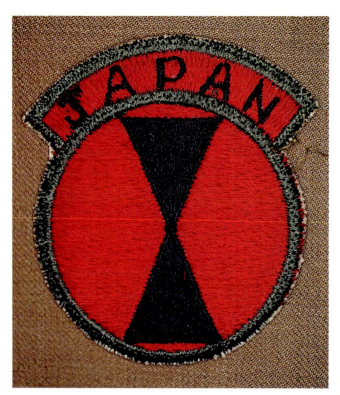

Fig. 7.29. Post World War II, Japan. FE 7th Division with integral "Japan" tab.

Fig. 7.30. Post World War II. ME on felt nickname tab.

Fig. 7.31. Post World War II, Japan. FE tab.

Fig. 7.32. Post World War II, Korea. Collar and shoulder strap of fatigue uniform. Chaplain device HE, mini 7th Division patch ME on twill.

Figs. 7.33 and 7.34. Post World War II, Korea. 7th Division Artillery name tags, ME on twill.

Fig. 7.35. Post World War II, Korea. 7th Division, Korean Augmentation Troops US Army Training School. KATUSA's were Korean military personnel that served in US Army units.

Fig. 7.36. Post World War II, Korea. Patch worn by KATUSA's. ME on felt and applied felt.

Figs. 7.37 and 7.38. Post World War II, Korea. Enamel 7th Division pocket badges, clutch back. Other versions of this device feature a wreath around the outside much like a Combat Infantry Badge.

Fig. 8.1. World War I. Pair of unidentified 8th Division doughboys.

Fig. 8.2. World War I. Bullion on velvet.

Fig. 8.3. World War I. Bullion on wool.

Fig. 8.4. Interwar. Felt on felt.

Figs. 8.5 and 8.6. Interwar. Two variations of ME on wool.

Fig. 8.7. Interwar. HE on wool.

Figs. 8.8 and 8.9. Interwar. Two examples of ME on wool.

Fig. 8.10. World War II. Two examples of FE patches, one with an ODB and one without.

Fig. 8.11. World War II. Two examples of ODB patches.

Fig. 8.12. World War II, England. FE

Fig. 8.13. Post World War II, Japan. FE

Fig. 8.14. Post World War II, Germany. FE, ODB.

Fig. 8.15. Post World War II, Germany. Bullion on felt.

Fig. 8.16. Post World War II, Germany. Bullion on felt.

Fig. 8.17. Post World War II. 8th Division patch with integral Airborne tab worn by the Airborne component of the division circa 1958-1963. FE.

Figs. 8.18 and 8.19. Post World War II, Germany. Two different FE variations.

Fig. U.1. World War I. The 18th Division standing in the formation of its shoulder patch. Before the end of World War I many Divisions were in the process of forming in the United States. When the war ended these units were disbanded prior to being federalized and as such were never "Official" Divisions. Like their federalized cousins they had a wide range of different patch designs some of which rank among the scarcest of all World War I patches. Divisions of the same numeral designation formed later do not share lineage with these units.

Fig. U.2. World War I. 9th Division. Wool on wool.

Fig. U.3. World War I. 10th Division. Felt on felt.

Fig. U.4. World War I. 10th Division. ME on felt.

Figs. U.5 and U.6. World War I. 11th Division. Felt on felt.

Fig. U.7. World War I. Richard E. Lehrer's 12th Division shoulder patch. Felt on felt.

Fig. U.8. World War I. 12th Division. Felt on felt.

Fig. U.9. World War I. 12th Division. ME on felt.

Fig. U.10. World War I. 12th Division. Liberty Loan.

Fig. U.11. World War I. A very nice image of an unidentified 13th Division Doughboy.

Fig. U.12. World War I. 13th Division. Felt on felt.

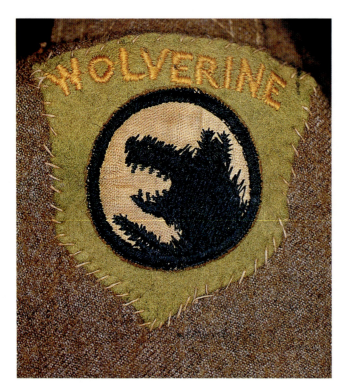

Fig. U.13. World War I. 14th Division. ME on cotton, applied to felt shield with ME lettering.

Fig. U.14. World War I. 14th Division. Felt on wool.

Fig. U.15. World War I. 14th Division. CS on felt.

Fig. U.16. World War I/Interwar. 14th Division. CS on felt applied to wool base.

Fig. U.17. Interwar. 14th Division. ME on wool.

Fig. U.18. World War I. 18th Division. CS on felt.

Fig. U.19. World War I. 18th Division. Felt on felt.

Fig. U.20. World War I. 19th Division. This patch was pinned to the jacket upside down by the doughboy owner because he received the patch just prior to being mustered out and was never instructed how to correctly place it on his uniform.

Fig. U.21. World War I. 19th Division alternate version. Felt on wool with HE details.

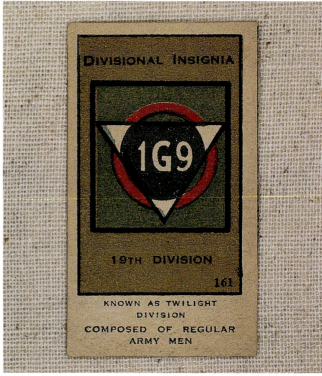

Fig. U.22. World War I. Cigarette card c.1919 showing another design of the 19th Division's shoulder patch.

Fig. 9.1. World War II. An unidentified 9th Division, 61st Regiment soldier.

Figs. 9.2 to 9.4. Interwar. Felt on wool.

Figs. 9.5 and 9.6. Interwar. ME on wool.

Fig. 9.7. Interwar. ET.

Fig. 9.8. Interwar. ME on wool with integral white detail.

Fig. 9.9. World War II. FE with hand added white detail.

Fig. 9.10. World War II. FE with hand added white details and miniature 61st Infantry Regiment DI.

Fig. 9.11. World War II. FE, ribbed variation.

Fig. 9.12. World War II, England. FE.

Fig. 9.13. Post World War II, Germany. HE on wool.

Fig. 9.14. Post World War II, Germany. HE on felt.

Fig. 9.15. Post World War II, Germany. HE on felt with bullion center.

Fig. 9.16. Post World War II, Germany. Felt on felt with HE detail and bullion center.

Fig. 9.17. Post World War II, Germany. FE patch with added bullion detail and border.

Fig. 9.18. Post World War II, Germany. HE on Officer's dark OD wool elastique with added bullion detail and border.

Fig. 9.19. Post World War II, Germany. HE on wool with bullion detail and border.

Fig. 9.20. Opposite: World War II/Post World War II. 1st Lieutenant George F. Bennethum, 9th Division Ordnance Officer. He is seen here relaxing on an unexploded 1600 Kilogram (4000 lbs.) German bomb. *Courtesy of Peter M. Bennethum.*

Fig. 9.21. Post World War II, Germany. 1st Lieutenant George F. Bennethum's 9th Division shoulder patch. Wool on wool with bullion detail and border. *Courtesy Peter M. Bennethum.*

Fig. 10.1. World War II. FE patch and tab.

Fig. 10.2. World War II/Post World War II. FE US made patch with theater added bullion.

Fig. 10.3. World War II, Italy. HE on twill and cotton.

Fig. 10.4. World War II, Italy. ME on ribbed satin base with HE lettering.

Fig. 10.5. World War II, Italy. HE on satin miniature patch. Miniature patches like this were usually worn on the garrison cap.

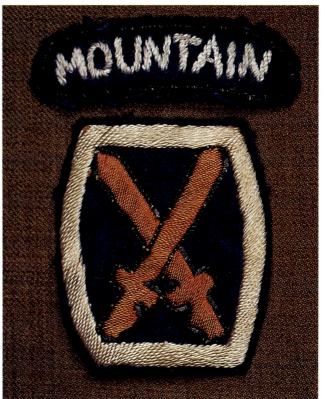

Fig. 10.6. World War II, Italy. HE on wool with bullion details.

Fig. 10.7. World War II, Italy. HE on wool with bullion lettering, detail and border.

Fig. 10.8. World War II, Italy. Incised leather, hand painted.

Fig. 10.9. World War II, Italy. Woven Mountain tab with wool backing.

Fig. 10.11. Post World War II. FE.

Fig. 10.10. Post World War II, Germany. HE on felt with bullion detail and border.

Fig. 10.12. Post World War II. ME on felt. Light blue background variation.

Fig. 10.13. Left: Post World War II. ME on felt patch. FE tab.

Fig. 10.14. Post World War II, Germany. FE Patch and tab.

Fig. 10.15. World War II. Crossed skis pin worn by 10th Mountain Division soldiers in lieu of the standard "US" collar brass.

Fig. 10.16. World War II. Crossed skis pin worn by the 10th Division, 85th Infantry Regiment.

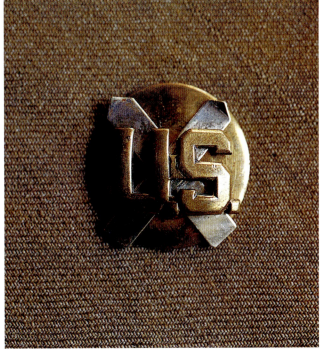

Fig. 10.17. Post World War II. Crossed skis enlisted disc. This example was made by Gemsco, NY. Clutch back.

Fig. 11.1. World War II. FE. Short tab variation.

Fig. 11.2. World War II. FE. Tall tab variation with light red background.

Fig. 11.3. Post World War II, Japan. ME on wool.

Fig. 11.4. Post World War II, Japan. HE on wool.

Fig. 11.5. Post World War II, Japan. HE on silk with quilted background and bullion separation between patch and tab.

Fig. 11.6. Post World War II, Japan. Painted insignia removed from an Army suitcase.

Fig. 11.7. Post World War II, Japan. Bullion on wool.

Fig. 11.8. Post World War II, Japan. Bullion on wool applied to cloth base.

Fig. 11.9. Post World War II, Japan. Bullion on silk.

Fig. 11.10. Post World War II, Japan. Bullion on silk quilted background.

Fig. 11.11. Post World War II, Japan. Painted patch type DI. Stickpin.

Figs. 11.12 and 11.13. Post World War II, Japan. Enamel patch type DI. Screwback.

Fig. 11.14. Post World War II, Germany. FE.

Fig. 12.1. Interwar, Philippines. Twill applied to cotton shield.

Fig. 12.2. Interwar. Felt on felt.

Fig. 12.3. Interwar/World War II. ME on felt.

Figs. 12.4 and 12.5. World War II. FE, ODB.

Fig. 12.6. World War II. FE. Ribbed variation.

Fig. 13.1. World War II. FE, ODB.

Fig. 13.2. World War II. FE, blue border.

Fig. 13.3. World War II. 13th Airborne Division Christmas Card.

Fig. 13.4. Post World War II, Germany. FE.

Fig. 17.1. World War II. FE with integral tab.

Fig. 17.2. World War II. FE. "ripple" variation.

Fig. 17.3. World War II. FE. "ripple" variation with opposed claw. The so called "opposed claw" is any 17th Airborne Division variation where the two center claws face each other.

Fig. 17.4. World War II. FE. Opposed claw.

Fig. 17.5. World War II. FE. Opposed claw with integral tab on green base material. This variation features a "split" in the leg feathers.

Fig. 17.6. World War II. FE. Opposed claw with integral tab and split variation on black base material.

Fig. 17.7. World War II. FE. Black border variation. Of special note is the "fitted" Airborne tab.

Fig. 17.8. World War II, England. FE. Patch with ME on wool tab.

Fig. 17.9. Post World War II, Germany. Woven patch and tab.

Fig. 17.10. Post World War II, Germany. Reverse of woven patch.

Fig. 17.11. Post World War II, Germany. FE.

Fig. 17.12. World War II/Post World War II, TM?. HE on wool.

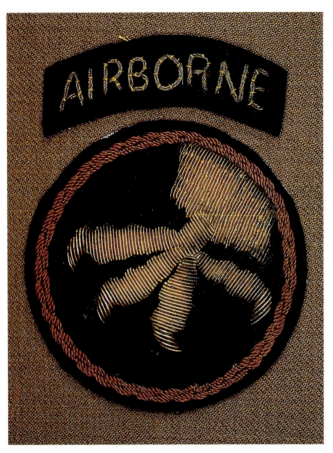

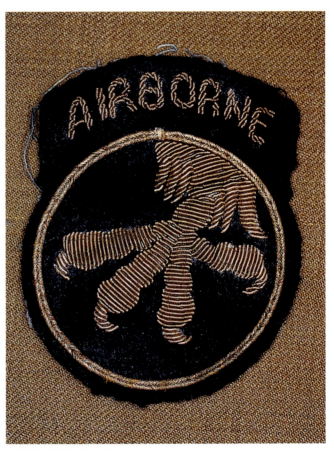

Fig. 17.13. Post World War II, Germany. Lt. Col. A.L. Bell. Bullion on wool.

Fig. 17.14. World War II, England. Colonel Lewis R. Good. Bullion on wool. *Courtesy of Peter M. Bennethum.*

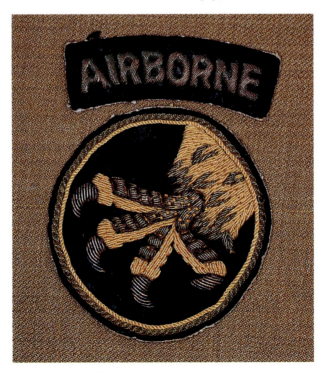

Fig. 17.15. Post World War II, Germany. HE on wool with bullion details, border and bullion tab. *Courtesy of Pete Bennethum.*

Fig. 23.1. World War II. FE.

Fig. 23.2. World War II. FE. Unusual variation in which star pattern is reversed.

Fig. 23.3. Post World War II, Germany. FE.

Fig. 23.4. Post World War II, Germany. Bullion on felt applied to wool base.

Fig. 24.1. Interwar. Soldiers of the Hawaiian Division standing in formation of their shoulder patch.

Fig. 24.2. Interwar. Felt on felt with cotton tape edge.

Fig. 24.5. Interwar. Another variation of a felt on felt with tape edge patch.

Figs. 24.3 and 24.4. Interwar. Front and back of a felt on felt with tape edge 24th Division patch. This is one style of backing device that can be found for this patch. The device facilitated quick removal from the tropical uniform for laundering.

Fig. 24.6. Interwar. Felt on felt with a black felt base.

Fig. 24.7. World War II. FE OBD.

Figs. 24.8 and 24.9. Post World War II, Germany. Two different variations of HE on felt with bullion details and border.

Figs. 24.10 to 24.15. Post World War II, Japan. Six different examples of FE silk 24th Division patches.

Fig. 24.14

Fig. 24.15

Fig. 24.16. Post World War II, Japan/Korea. HE on wool.

Fig. 24.17. Post World War II, Japan. Felt on felt with bullion details.

Fig. 24.18. Post World War II, Japan. Felt on felt with bullion details.

Fig. 24.19. Post World War II, Japan. Felt on felt with bullion details and HE silk border.

Fig. 24.20. Post World War II, Japan. Silk leaf applied to felt with bullion detail.

Fig. 24.21. Post World War II, Japan. Fully HE with bullion detail.

Figs. 24.22 and 24.23. Post World War II, Japan. Two different fully HE 24th Divisions with quilted backgrounds and bullion details.

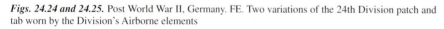

Figs. 24.24 and 24.25. Post World War II, Germany. FE. Two variations of the 24th Division patch and tab worn by the Division's Airborne elements

Fig. 24.26. Post World War II, Germany. FE. Another variety of a German made patch and a U.S. made "Germany" tab.

Figs. 25.1 to 25.4. Post World War II, Japan. FE.

Figs. 25.5 and 25.6. Post World War II, Japan. HE on felt.

Fig. 25.7. Post World War II, Japan. HE on wool.

Fig. 25.8. Post World War II, Japan. HE on silk.

Fig. 25.9. Post World War II, Japan. HE on wool with bullion detail.

Fig. 25.10. Post World War II, Japan. Bullion on wool.

Figs. 25.11 to 25.14. Post World War II, Japan. Four different bullion on felt variations.

Fig. 25.13

Fig. 25.14

Fig. 25.15. Post World War II, Japan/Korea. Bullion on wool with integral "Korea" tab.

Fig. 25.16. Post World War II, Japan/Korea. HE on wool "Korea" tab for the 25th Division.

Fig. 25.17. Post World War II, Germany. FE.

Fig. 25.18. Post World War II, Japan. 25th Division patch type DI, screwback

Fig. 25.19. Post World War II, Japan. Another 25th patch type DI, clutchback marked "Made in Japan".

Fig. 25.20. Post World War II, Japan. HE DI size 25th Division patch, pinback.

Fig. 26.1. World War I. An unidentified 26th Division, 103rd Infantry Regiment NCO wearing an applied construction patch. Notice the small "YD" pin on his garrison cap.

Figs. 26.2 and 26.3. World War I. Wool on wool.

Fig. 26.4. World War I. Unidentified 26th Division doughboy with an applied construction patch.

Fig. 26.5. World War I. HE on wool.

Fig. 26.6. World War I. ME on wool.

Fig. 26.7. World War I. 1st Lieutenant F.T. Bradford, 101st Infantry Regiment. ME on wool.

Fig. 26.8. World War I. ME on felt.

Fig. 26.9. World War I. Liberty Loan.

Fig. 26.10. Interwar. HE on Officer's dark OD wool elastique.

Fig. 26.11. Interwar. ME on wool disc.

Fig. 26.12. Interwar. ME on wool.

Fig. 26.13. Interwar. ME on Officer's dark OD wool elastique.

Fig. 26.14. Interwar. ME on light weight khaki cotton.

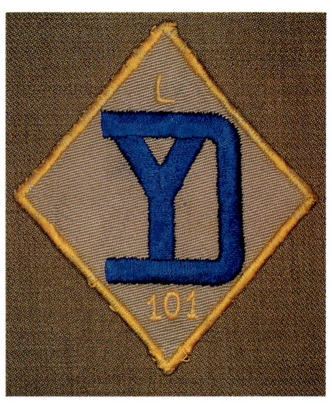

Fig. 26.15. Interwar. 26th Division, 101st Infantry Regiment, Company L. TW with hand added numbers, letter and border.

Fig. 26.16. Interwar. TW.

Fig. 26.17. Interwar/World War II. TW, ODB.

Fig. 26.18. Interwar/World War II. ME on green twill with ODB.

Fig. 26.19. World War II. FE.

Fig. 26.20. World War II, England. FE miniature garrison cap patch.

Fig. 26.21. World War II/Post World War II, TM. Very oddly constructed with applied "YD" on zig-zag embroidered background.

Fig. 26.22. Post World War II, Germany. FE

Fig. 26.23. Post World War II, Germany. HE on wool with bullion detail and border.

Fig. 26.25. Post World War II, Germany. 26th Division nickname tab. FE.

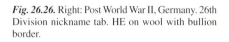

Fig. 26.24. Post World War II, Germany. HE on felt with bullion details and border.

Fig. 26.26. Right: Post World War II, Germany. 26th Division nickname tab. HE on wool with bullion border.

Inside the image: © MOLE and THOMAS / 915 Medinah Bldg. / CHICAGO, ILL. / March 18-'19.

LIVING INSIGNIA / of the / TWENTY-SEVENTH DIVISION / "NEW YORK'S OWN" / Breakers of the Hindenburg Line / Formed of 10,000 Officers and Enlisted Men

Fig. 27.1. World War I. "Living Insignia", the 27th Division in the formation of their shoulder patch.

Fig. 27.2. World War I. Wool tape applied to wool with HE stars.

Fig. 27.3. World War I. CS on wool.

Fig. 27.4. World War I. HE on wool.

Fig. 27.5. World War I. ME on wool.

Fig. 27.6. World War I. Liberty Loan.

Fig. 27.7. World War I. 27th Division welcome home ribbon. Woven.

Fig. 27.8. Interwar. Unidentified 27th Division Sergeant.

Fig. 27.9. Right: Interwar. ME on wool.

Fig. 27.10. Interwar. HE on wool.

Figs. 27.11 and 27.12. Above and below: Interwar. ME on wool.

Fig. 27.13. World War II. Interwar. TW.

Fig. 27.14. World War II. FE, ODB. This example has a red circle against the OD border.

Fig. 27.15. World War II. FE, ODB. This example has a black circle against the OD border.

Fig. 27.16. World War II. FE. Note the different "NY" monogram overlay of the two patches.

Fig. 27.17. Post World War II, Japan. FE.

Fig. 27.18. Post World War II, Japan. HE on wool with quilted background.

Fig. 28.1. World War I. Unidentified 28th Division doughboy with a cut out style patch.

Fig. 28.3. World War I. Die cut wool.

Fig. 28.2. World War I. Unidentified 28th Division Engineer wearing a cut out style patch.

Fig. 28.4. World War I. Wool on wool.

Fig. 28.5. World War I. Unidentified 28th Division, 107th Field Artillery Regiment doughboy with a wool on wool patch.

Fig. 28.6. World War I. Wool on wool.

Fig. 28.7. World War I. Felt on wool with stamped numbers.

Fig. 28.8. World War I. ME on felt.

Fig. 28.9. World War I/Interwar. Vic Levin Jr. and Sr. posing with the 28th Division, 103rd Engineer Band's base drum.

Fig. 28.10. Interwar. Felt on wool.

Figs. 28.11 and 28.12. Above and below: Interwar. ME on wool.

Fig. 28.13. World War II. Comparison of shoulder and overseas cap patches. FE.

Fig. 28.14. World War II. FE, oversize variation.

Fig. 28.15. World War II. FE, ODB.

Fig. 28.16. Post World War II, Germany. Bullion on felt.

Fig. 29.1. World War I. A very nice group photo of 29th Division doughboys.

Figs. 29.2 and 29.3. World War I. Two variations of HE on wool.

Fig. 29.4. World War I. Wool on wool.

Fig. 29.5. World War I. ME on felt.

Fig. 29.6. World War I. ME on wool. Of note is the reverse direction of the divisional symbol.

Fig. 29.8. Interwar. Felt on felt.

Fig. 29.7. Interwar. Woven reunion ribbon for the 114th Infantry Regiment.

Figs. 29.9 and 29.10. Interwar. ME on wool, two different variations.

Fig. 29.11. Interwar. ME on Officer's dark OD wool elastique.

Fig. 29.12. Interwar. ME on dark blue wool for wear on the dress uniform.

Fig. 29.13. World War II. FE.

Fig. 29.14. World War II. FE with reversed design.

Fig. 29.15. World War II, English. FE.

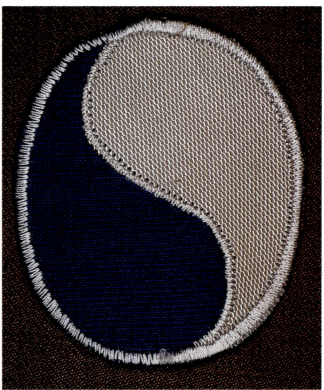

Fig. 29.16. Post World War II, Germany. Satin like material applied to twill base material.

Fig. 29.17. World War II/Post World War II, TM? ME on felt.

Fig. 29.18. Post World War II, Germany. HE bullion on twill base. The grey side is actually bullion that has oxidized.

Fig. 30.1. World War I. 30th Division doughboy wearing the patch World War I style. Initially the division wore their patch horizontally. The proper way to wear the patch is vertically. One story relayed to the author has the 30th's commanding General's aide sewing the patch on the General's uniform incorrectly. This lead to the rest of the division following suit.

Fig. 30.2. World War I. HE on wool.

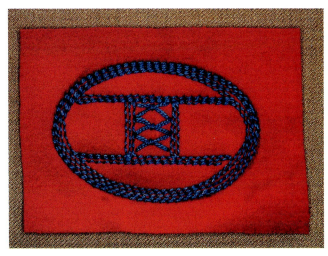

Fig. 30.3. World War I. CS on red wool background.

Figs. 30.4 to 30.7. World War I. HE on wool.

Fig. 30.8. World War I. Liberty Loan.

Fig. 30.9. World War I. Liberty Loan with light red background.

Fig. 30.10. Interwar. ME on wool.

Fig. 30.11. Interwar. ME on felt.

Figs. 30.12 and 30.13. World War II. FE, ODB.

Fig. 30.14. World War II. FE, ODB with pink background.

Fig. 30.15. World War II. FE, red border.

Fig. 30.16. World War II. FE with double blue border.

Fig. 30.17. World War II. FE with added ordnance garrison cap piping.

Fig. 30.18. World War II, England. FE.

Fig. 30.19. World War II/Post World War II, TM. FE. This patch features an unusual woven like background with embroidered details.

Fig. 30.20. World War II/Post World War II, TM. Similar to ***30.19*** with red border.

Fig. 30.21. World War II/Post World War II, TM. Similar to ***30.20*** with light blue design.

Fig. 30.22. World War II/Post World War II, TM. ME on satin like material.

Fig. 30.23. Post World War II, Germany. FE.

Fig. 30.24. Post World War II, Japan. FE.

Fig. 31.1. World War I. Unidentified 31st Division doughboy.

Fig. 31.2. World War I. Bullion on wool.

Figs. 31.3 and 31.4. Above and below: World War I. Felt on felt. This is the alternate design for the 31st Division in World War I.

Fig. 31.5. World War I. ME on felt.

Fig. 31.6. World War I. Liberty Loan.

Fig. 31.7. Interwar. Felt on felt.

Fig. 31.8. Interwar. Felt on wool.

Figs. 31.9 and 31.10. Interwar. ME on wool.

Fig. 31.11. Interwar. ME on wool. White field variation.

Fig. 31.12. Interwar. TW.

Fig. 31.13. Interwar. ME on felt.

Figs. 31.14 and 31.15. World War II. FE, ODB.

Figs. 31.16 and 31.17. World War II. FE, White border variation.

Fig. 31.18. Post World War II, Germany. FE.

Fig. 31.19. Post World War II, Germany. HE on felt.

Fig. 32.1. World War I. Unidentified 32nd Division doughboy. Of special interest in this photo are the 3rd Army and trench mortar patches.

Fig. 32.2. World War I. Felt on wool.

Fig. 32.3. World War I. Wool arrow on an odd woven background.

Fig. 32.4. World War I. Felt on wool. This unusual variation features a blue felt edge to the arrow and ME feather detail.

Fig. 32.5. World War I. Cotton cloth with wool backing and HE silk border.

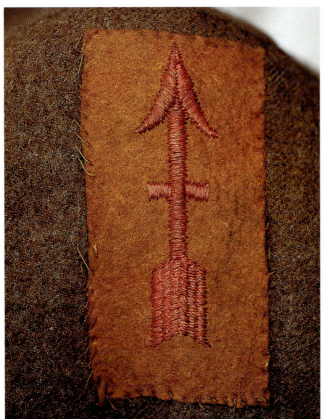

Fig. 32.6. Left: World War I. ME on felt.

Fig. 32.7. Above left: World War I. ME on wool.

Fig. 32.8. Left: World War I. Unidentified doughboy, 32nd Division, Army of Occupation.

Fig. 32.9. Above right: World War I. 32nd Division, Army of Occupation. Liberty Loan 32nd Division patch and ME on felt 3rd Army patch.

Figs. 32.10 to 32.13. Interwar. ME on wool.

Fig. 32.14. Interwar. ME on wool with ME border.

Fig. 32.15. Interwar. ME on Officer's dark OD wool elastique.

Fig. 32.16. Interwar. ME on wool.

Fig. 32.17. Interwar. ME on dark blue wool.

Fig. 32.18. Interwar. TW.

Fig. 32.19. World War II. FE, ODB.

Fig. 32.20. World War II. FE.

Figs. 32.21 and 32.22. Post World War II, Japan. Wool on wool.

Fig. 32.23. Post World War II, Japan. Cotton cloth on wool.

Fig. 32.24. Post World War II, TM. Felt with ME border.

Fig. 32.25. Post World War II, Germany. HE on wool with bullion detail.

Fig. 32.26. Post World War II, Japan. HE in a quilted pattern on World War II Japanese Army Officer quality wool.

Fig. 32.27. Post World War II, Japan. HE on TW with ODB.

Fig. 32.28. Post World War II, Japan. HE with a quilted field.

Fig. 32.29. Right: Post World War II, Japan. HE on silk with a quilted field and bullion detail.

Fig. 32.30. Far right: Post World War II, Japan. Enameled patch type DI. Pinback.

Figs. 33.1 and 33.2. World War I. Two unidentified 33rd Division doughboys wearing bullion patches.

Fig. 33.3. World War I. Bullion on wool, similar to the patches being worn in ***Figs. 33.1*** and ***33.2.***

Fig. 33.4. Right: World War I. Private Lawrence Lindberg, "Mascot of the 122nd Machine Gun Battalion" wearing a bullion tape style 33rd Division patch.

Fig. 33.5. World War I. Bullion tape on wool.

Fig. 33.6. World War I. ME on felt.

Fig. 33.7. World War I. ME on wool.

Fig. 33.8. Interwar. ME on felt.

Fig. 33.9. Interwar. ME on felt with HE border.

Fig. 33.10. Interwar. ME on wool.

Fig. 33.11. World War II. 33rd Division, 130th Infantry Regiment Corporal wearing a FE, ODB shoulder patch.

Fig. 33.12. World War II. FE, ODB.

Fig. 33.13. World War II. FE.

Fig. 33.14. Post World War II, Japan. Fully HE in silk with Bullion border.

Fig. 33.15. Post World War II, Japan. Bullion on wool.

Fig. 33.16. Post World War II, Japan. Bullion on felt with bullion edge.

Fig. 33.17. Post World War II, Japan. Bullion on felt with bullion border applied to a wool base.

Fig. 34.1. World War I. The 34th Division standing in the formation of their patch. During World War I the Division was known as the "Sandstorm" Division.

Fig. 34.2. World War I. Unidentified engineer with an interesting variation of the 34th's shoulder patch, applied construction with a white or light colored background.

Fig. 34.3. World War I. A group of doughboys, one with another odd variation of the 34th patch. The patch is applied to a circular background with a bullion stripe at the bottom.

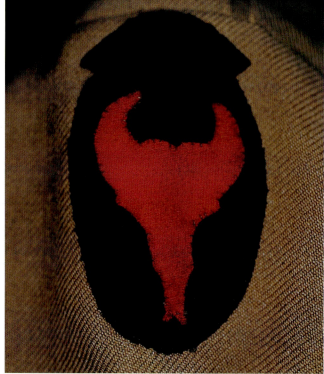

Figs. 34.4 and 34.5. World War I. Wool on wool.

Fig. 34.6. World War I. HE on wool with bullion border and numbers. Smaller over seas cap size patch.

Fig. 34.7. World War I. Liberty Loan.

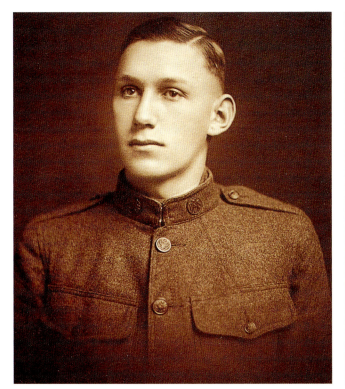

Figs. 34.8 and 34.9. World War I. An unidentified doughboy from Co. C, 109th Engineer Regiment, 34th Division and his ME on felt patch. Like the 2nd Division, the 34th occasionally employed a color coded system. While further research in needed to uncover the identity of some of these colors, it can be said with certainty that during World War I the 109th Engineer Regiment utilized a green border.

Fig. 34.10. World War I. PFC F. Noerenberg, Co. D, 109th Engineer Regiment. Wool on wool.

Fig. 34.11. World War I. Lt. H.C. Headley, Co. B, 109th Engineer Regiment. Wool on wool with a bullion soutache border. Officer's patches for this regiment were apparently differentiated from those of enlisted personnel by the addition of a bullion border. Other examples of this patch identified to Officers have been observed.

Fig. 34.12. Interwar. Felt on felt.

Fig. 34.13. Right: Interwar. ME on felt.

Fig. 34.14. Interwar/World War II. FE on felt.

Figs. 34.15 and 34.16. Above and below: World War II. FE, ODB.

Fig. 34.17. World War II, TM?. FE with a light OD or grey border.

Figs. 34.18 and 34.19. World War II, Italy. Front and reverse of a woven 34th Division.

Fig. 34.20. World War II, Italy. HE on felt.

Figs. 34.21 and 34.22. World War II, Italy. HE on wool with HE border.

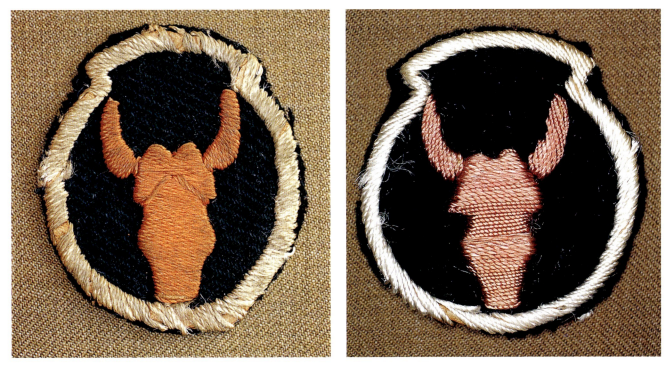

Figs. 34.23 and 34.24. World War II, Italy. HE on wool with white border.

Fig. 34.25. World War II, Italy. Felt on wool with HE green border.

Fig. 34.26. World War II, Italy. HE on wool with white border garrison cap patch.

Figs. 34.27 and 34.28. World War II, Italy. HE on wool with bullion border.

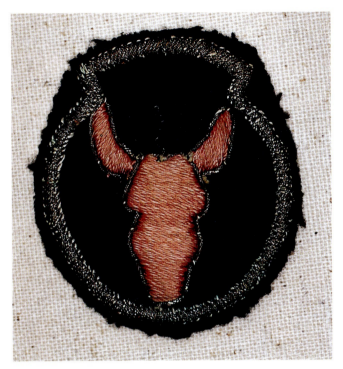

Fig. 34.29. World War II, Italy. HE on wool with bullion details and border.

Fig. 34.30. World War II, Italy. HE patch on cotton with HE on wool "Red Bull" tab and bullion "Italy" tab. During World War II the division was known as the "Red Bull Division".

Fig. 34.31. World War II, Italy. HE patch on wool with HE on wool with bullion border tab.

Fig. 34.32. World War II, Italy. HE patch on satin applied to wool base with HE on wool with bullion border tab. Of special note is the "arrow" configuration of the tab.

Fig. 34.33. World War II, Italy. Wool on wool patch with bullion detail and border, HE on wool with bullion border tab.

Fig. 34.34. Post World War II, Germany. HE on wool with cello cord edge.

Fig. 34.35. Post World War II, Germany. Red bullion on wool.

Fig. 35.1. World War I. An unidentified doughboy of the 35th Infantry Division wearing the all black patch of the 70th Infantry Brigade. The 35th Division's patch, a likeness of the Santa Fe Cross, is divided into four center and four outer quadrants. The color combinations in these areas are used to designate different units within the division. This system was used from World War I into the Interwar period.

Fig. 35.2. World War I. 35th Division, Headquarters Troop. ME on wool.

Fig. 35.3. World War I. 35th Division, 70th Infantry Brigade. HE on wool.

Fig. 35.4. World War I. 35th Division, 137th Infantry Regiment. ME on wool. It should be noted that traditionally the odd colored quadrant is in the top left position. This patch was removed from a uniform with the colored quadrant in the lower right position. The uniform was accompanied by a helmet with the divisional insignia painted in the same manner and it is illustrated this way on the cover of the Regimental history.

Fig. 35.5. World War I. 35th Division, 128th Field Artillery Regiment. Wool on wool.

Fig. 35.6. World War I. 35th Division, 128th Field Artillery Regiment? This may be a variation for the 128th F.A. Regiment with blue outer quadrants or another unit entirely. ME on felt.

Fig. 35.7. World War I. An unidentified doughboy possibly of the 129th Field Artillery Regiment. One yellow quadrant with all others red.

Fig. 35.8. World War I. An unidentified doughboy of the 35th Division, 130th Field Artillery Regiment. One white quadrant with all others red. As evidenced from **Figs. 35.5, 35.7** and **35.8** one can see how a standardized quadrant policy was not always adhered to.

Fig. 35.9. World War I. 35th Division, 130th Machine Gun Battalion. ME on felt.

Fig. 35.10. World War I. 35th Division, 130th Machine Gun Battalion? ME on felt. This example may be a variation for the 130th M.G. Battalion with yellow outer quadrants or for another unit entirely.

Fig. 35.11. World War I. 35th Division, unidentified unit, possibly the 129th Machine Gun Battalion. HE on wool.

Fig. 35.12. World War I/Interwar. 35th Division, unidentified unit.

Fig. 35.13. Interwar. 35th Division Headquarters Troop.

Fig. 35.14. Interwar. 35th Division, 70th Infantry Brigade. ME on wool.

Fig. 35.15. Interwar. 35th Division, 128th Field Artillery Regiment. ME on wool.

Fig. 35.16. Interwar. 35th Division, 128th Field Artillery Regiment. TW.

Fig. 35.17. Interwar. 35th Division, 130th Field Artillery Regiment. ME on wool.

Fig. 35.18. Interwar. Dark blue variation. ME on wool.

Figs. 35.19 and 35.20. Above and below: Interwar. Light blue variation. ME on wool.

Fig. 35.21. Interwar. ME on Officer's dark OD wool elastique.

Fig. 35.22. World War II. FE.

Fig. 35.23. Post World War II, Germany. Bullion on felt.

Fig. 35.24. Post World War II, Germany. Bullion on felt with bullion edge.

Fig. 36.1. World War I. An unidentified doughboy with a shoulder and garrison cap 36th Division patch.

Fig. 36.2. World War I. ME on felt.

Fig. 36.3. World War I. ME on wool.

Fig. 36.4. World War I. ME on felt.

Fig. 36.5. World War I. 36th Division Doughboy with an unusual saw tooth edge shoulder patch.

Figs. 36.6 and 36.7. World War I. HE on wool.

Fig. 36.8. World War I. Bullion on wool applied to wool background.

Fig. 36.9. World War I. Alternate 36th Division variation, representing the "Star" in the "Lone Star State" of Texas, the unit's home area. Wool on wool with ME border.

Figs. 36.10 and 36.11. 2 Different Liberty Loan variations.

Figs. 36.12 to 36.14. Interwar. ME on wool.

Fig. 36.15. Interwar. ME on wool with embroidered border.

Fig. 36.16. Interwar. ME on wool with embroidered green border.

Fig. 36.17. Interwar. ME on Officer's dark OD wool elastique.

Figs. 36.18 and 36.19. Interwar. Embroidered on twill folded edge.

Figs. 36.20 and 36.21. Interwar. ME on twill with embroidered border.

Figs. 36.22 to 36.25. World War II. FE.

Fig. 36.26. World War II, Italy. Woven.

Fig. 36.27. World War II, Italy. HE on satin.

Fig. 36.28. World War II, Italy. HE on wool with Bullion border.

Fig. 36.29. World War II, England. FE.

Fig. 36.30. Post World War II, Germany. ME on cotton.

Fig. 36.31. Post World War II, Germany. ME on cotton with OD border.

Fig. 36.32. Post World War II, Germany. ME on cotton with grey border.

Fig. 36.33. Post World War II, Germany. ME on felt with OD border.

Fig. 36.34. Post World War II, Germany. FE, yellow "T" and border variation.

Fig. 36.35. Post World War II, Germany. ME.

Fig. 36.36. Post World War II, Germany. HE on bullion laced cloth applied to wool background.

Fig. 36.37. Post World War II, Germany. Bullion on felt with bullion cord edge.

Fig. 37.1. World War I. An unidentified Distinguished Service Cross winner of the 37th Division.

Fig. 37.2. World War I. Wool on wool.

Fig. 37.3. World War I. An unidentified 37th Division doughboy with a fully hand embroidered patch.

Fig. 37.4. World War I. An unidentified 37th Division doughboy with a felt on felt patch with "37" embroidered in the center.

Fig. 37.5. Right: World War I. An unidentified 37th Division doughboy with a ME patch.

Fig. 37.6. World War I. This is the same style patch as worn in ***Fig. 37.5.*** ME on felt.

Fig. 37.7. World War I. ME on felt.

Fig. 37.8. World War I. Liberty Loan.

Fig. 37.9. World War I. Alternate World War I design for the 37th Division. ME on felt.

Fig. 37.10. World War I. M1910 Haversack decorated with the 37th Division's patch.

Fig. 37.11. Interwar. Cotton on cotton construction.

Fig. 37.13. Interwar. CS on felt applied to a wool base.

Fig. 37.12. Interwar. Felt on felt applied to a wool base.

Fig. 37.14. Interwar. ME on felt applied to a wool base. A twill patch with this style of center embroidery also exists.

Figs. 37.15 and 37.16. Interwar. ME on wool.

Fig. 37.17. Interwar. ME on Officer's dark OD wool elastique.

Fig. 37.18. Interwar. TW.

Fig. 37.19. Interwar. Felt on felt.

Fig. 37.20. Interwar/World War II. FE with integral "37" at center.

Fig. 37.21. World War II. FE, ODB.

Fig. 37.22. World War II. FE.

Fig. 38.1. World War I. An unidentified 38th Division doughboy and a friend.

Fig. 38.2. World War I. Felt on felt.

Fig. 38.3. World War I. HE on felt.

Fig. 38.4. World War I. ME on wool.

Figs. 38.5 and 38.6. World War I/Interwar. ME on wool.

Fig. 38.7. Interwar. ME on wool.   ***Fig. 38.8.*** Interwar. ME on wool with embroidered border.

Fig. 38.9. Interwar. TW.

Figs. 38.10 and 38.11. Interwar. ME on wool.

Fig. 38.12. World War II. A 38th Division GI wearing a FE patch.

Fig. 38.13. World War II. FE.

Fig. 38.14. World War II. FE, reversed shield variation (red first).

Fig. 38.15. World War II. FE, ribbed background variation.

Fig. 38.16. World War II. FE, khaki tan border variation.

Fig. 38.17. Post World War II, TM. Bullion on felt applied to a felt base.

Figs. 39.1 and 39.2. World War I. HE on wool.

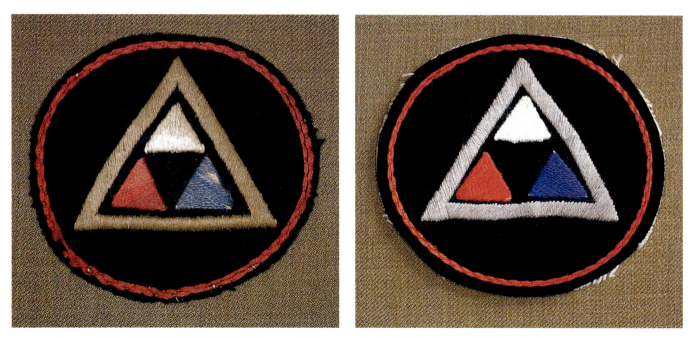

Figs. 39.3 and 39.4. World War I. HE on wool. These two variations feature an unusual border embroidery pattern.

Fig. 39.5. Interwar. Felt on felt applied to a wool base.

Fig. 39.6. Interwar/World War II. Felt on felt with a machine embroidered OD border. This patch is pictured in a color insert from the *Philadelphia Inquirer*'s April 23, 1942 issue. *Reprinted with permission from the Philadelphia Inquirer.*

Fig. 39.7. World War II. FE, ribbed background, slightly oversized patch.

Fig. 39.8. Post World War II, TM. HE on felt. It appears that there was once a border on this patch that was removed.

Fig. 40.1. Post World War II, Japan. A very nice portrait of an unidentified 40th Division soldier executed on silk.

Figs. 40.2 and 40.3. World War I. ME on felt.

Fig. 40.4. World War I. Bullion on wool.

Fig. 40.5. World War I. Bullion on velvet.

Fig. 40.6. World War I. ME on felt overseas cap patch.

Figs. 40.7 and 40.8. Above and below: Interwar. ME on felt.

Fig. 40.9. World War II. FE. The embroidery pattern of the sun is very similar to **Fig. 40.8.**

Figs. 40.10 and 40.11. World War II. FE, ODB.

Fig. 40.12. World War II. FE, with woven like background.

Fig. 40.13. World War II/Post World War II. FE. A standard U.S. made World War II patch with HE details.

Fig. 40.14. Post World War II. An unidentified Korean War era 40th Division Tech. Sergeant.

Fig. 40.15. Post World War II, Japan. FE.

Fig. 40.16. Post World War II, Japan. HE on silk with HE border.

Figs. 40.17 and 40.18. Post World War II, Japan. Bullion on felt.

Fig. 40.19. Post World War II, Japan. Bullion on felt with bullion border.

Fig. 40.20. Post World War II, Japan/Korea. Bullion on wool with bullion border.

Fig. 40.22. Post World War II. During the Korean War the 40th Division wore different two variations of its shoulder patch. The standard blue square worn in a diamond fashion, and a larger lozenge style patch with a blazing sun at the center that was usually worn with a "Ball of Fire" nickname tab. FE.

Fig. 40.21. Post World War II, Germany. Bullion on felt with bullion cord border.

Fig. 40.24. Post World War II, Japan. FE.

Fig. 40.23. Post World War II. FE, U.S. made patch and a FE Japanese made tab.

Fig. 40.25. Post World War II, Japan. FE patch and tab.

Fig. 40.26. Post World War II, Korea. HE on wool.

Fig. 40.27. Post World War II, Japan. Bullion on felt applied to a wool base.

Figs. 40.28 and 40.29. Above and below: Post World War II, Japan. FE. A close up of two slightly different Japanese made tabs. A U.S. made version of this tab also exists.

Fig. 40.30. Post World War II, Japan. Enamel patch type DI. Screwback.

Bibliography

Angolia, LTC (Ret.) John R. *Cloth Insignia of the SS*. San Jose, California: R. James Bender Publishing, 1983.

Angolia, John R. and Adolf Schlicht. *Uniforms & Traditions of the German Army 1933-1945 Vol. 1*. San Jose, California: R. James Bender Publishing, 1984.

Britton, Jack and George Washington Jr.. *U.S. Military Shoulder Patches of the United States Armed Forces*. Tulsa, Oklahoma: M.C.N. Press, 1985.

Emerson, William K. *Encyclopedia of United States Army Insignia and Uniforms*. Norman: University of Oklahoma Press, 1996.

Lewis, Kenneth. *Doughboy to GI: U.S. Army Clothing and Equipment 1900-1945*. West Midlands, England: Norman D. Landing Publishing, 1993.

Morgan, George O. and Mark Warren. *Shoulder Sleeve Insignia of the A.E.F. 1917-1919*. Keokuk, Iowa: Hill Printing Co., 1986.

Phillips, Stanley S. *Civil War Corps Badges and Other Related Awards, Badges, Medals of the Period*. Lanham, Maryland: S.S. Phillips and Assoc., 1982.

Rottman, Gordon. *U.S. Army Airborne 1940-90*. London, England: Osprey Publishing Ltd., 1990.

Schulz, P.J., H. Otoupalik, and D. Gordon. *World One Collectors Handbook Vols. 1 & 2*. Missoula, Montana: GOS Publishing Inc., 1988.

Smith and Pelz. *Shoulder Sleeve Insignia of the U.S. Armed Forces 1941-1945*. N.p., 1981.

Stanton, Shelby. *U.S. Army Uniforms of The Cold War 1948-1973*. Mechanicsburg, Pennsylvania: Stackpole Books, 1994.

Stanton, Shelby. *U.S. Army Uniforms of The Korean War*. Harrisburg, Pennsylvania: Stackpole Books, 1992.

Stanton, Shelby. *U.S. Army Uniforms of World War 2*. Harrisburg, Pennsylvania: Stackpole Books, 1991.

Stanton, Shelby L. *World War II Order of Battle*. New York, New York: Galahad Books, 1984.

Windrow, Martin. *Waffen-SS*. London, England: Osprey Publishing Ltd., 1971.